THE THORN IN THE VERSE

POEMS

BY

JEAN HILL

Copyright © 2019. Jean Hill. All rights reserved

ISBN: 978-0-244-64885-8

Printed and Distributed by Lulu.com

First Published: November 2017

Second Edition

Other work by **Jean Hill**

The Sting In The Tale
Poems and Short Stories

The Lyric In The Lines

The Barb In The Rhyme
Poems to make you laugh and cry

and

Let's Smile Again
A Humorous Account of
Family Life in the Seventies

Available from: Lulu.com
or
Amazon

Pause for Poetry

HERE WE GO AGAIN

Well, would you believe it, my fourth book – poetry again this time. I can't believe I now have a little gang of faithful followers who have bought all my books and asked for more. What gluttons for punishment you are and how grateful I am to you. Without your actually wanting to read my books the muse would leave my shoulder and inspiration would die forever! I feel every reader is a friend and I love to hear from you.

It's been a particular pleasure for me to present my poems on Radio Berkshire and to so many social groups, and bookings continue throughout the year. After-dinner speaking which, five years ago, would have had me quaking in my stilettos, is a rewarding experience and an opportunity to meet so many wonderful people.

However ... presenting to a ladies' group one afternoon, I was confronted by a disgruntled participant who said she had "heard me before" and "I was awful". Apparently I was solely responsible for "the most depressing afternoon of her life". Feeling rather dejected but realising the show must go on, I went ahead and read the selection of humorous poems I had chosen for that particular group. Very soon after starting I caught her laughing and, the funnier my poems became, the more she laughed – until tears trickled down her face! She approached me afterwards. "I remember now dear" she said, "It wasn't you – the poet I listened to last time had fat legs!" I'm not sure what relieved me most – the fact I wasn't the 'awful depressing poet', or that I haven't got fat legs! That delightful lady was instantly forgiven.

My third book Let's Smile Again, a humorous reflection on family life in the 70's, was something of a gamble that worked and has been very successful – so many readers have identified with every word. My poetry books The Sting in the Tale, The Barb in the Rhyme, and now The Thorn in the Verse, continue the theme of mixing funny and topical poetry to make you laugh and cry. What would I call a fifth book? One of my more audacious readers suggested The Prick in the Poem. I don't think so! So many poems – so many lovely people. Thank you all once again. I hope you enjoy reading The Thorn in the Verse.

See – I haven't got fat legs!
(The rest of me might be a bit 'iffy')

ACKNOWLEDGEMENTS

Deborah and **Samantha**
for being so hugely supportive
in the practical production of this book.
Without your skill and patience it would
never have happened.

Sharon ... for continued encouragement.

Robin ... for the front cover photography.

Benjamin and **Jamie** ... for just being.

The talented members of Wokingham Library Poetry Group
for never-ending inspiration.

THANK-YOU ALL

Treasure This Moment

ACTION IN TRACTION

It was on a Monday morning
That the doctor came to call
And with all my bumps and bruises
Said it was a nasty fall

They've splinted up my fractures
Put all my joints in plaster
No stinting on the NHS
For this medical disaster

Sitting on my Stannah Stair Lift
Listening to my ghetto-blaster
I'd muddled up the buttons
Missed the brake and pressed 'go faster'

I was speeding up quite nicely
When it caught me unawares
Swerved and hurtled around the bend
Then flung me down the stairs

So now I'm out of action
And bandaged head to toe
With both my legs in traction
I've bought a bungalow

AUF WIEDERSEHEN PET
(2017)

On the twenty-ninth of March
The Brexit plan was triggered
It all seems very daunting
But guess Theresa has it figured

We say Goodbye to Germany
We're no longer in your circle
With your bratwurst and your sauerkraut
Auf Wiedersehen Frau Merkel

It's Au Revoir to French fries
No more frogs-legs or escargot
But we'll negotiate a booze cruise
And reject a wine embargo

It's Arrivederci Roma
And Italian ravioli
We don't want your spaghetti
And you can keep your minestrone

No more propping up the Greeks
'Though a trade deal we may barter
You can send sun-ripe tomatoes
But not your taramasalata

Now it's Adiós España
But Britain keeps Gibraltar
Remind Spain of the Falklands
And Galtieri's plan to alter

We had the referendum
'Though it's upset quite a few
It's 'Hello' wide world out there
And 'Goodbye' the EU

BEIGE COLOURED DAYS

Wetly glistening, the stone, I trace
Your name with gnarled and blue-veined hands
Mottled white finger tips read the letters
On the memorial – this monument to madness
To my beige coloured days and tears unshed
"Wait for me"
You said, you said

Amid sodden poppies, the brass-band plays
And I hear echoes of the village carousel
Where horses grazed in fields now violated
With urban sprawl and shopping malls
I hold fast to my one silvered thread
I was once loved
You said, you said

You went the day the sun shone through
A misty dawn when the birds still sang
And church bells pealed their evensong
And wheat fields fanned with golden blush
When sun-sets gloried tones of red
"I'll come back, we'll wed"
You said, you said

A boy to adventure not understanding
In jaunty cap and hair shorn short
Village lads together, the Pals Brigade
With boots that sparked on cobbled stones
Over by Christmas, with Jerries fled
"Marching home victorious"
You said, you said

Your letters came with foreign stamps
Anguish between each censored line
My fresh-faced beau of tender years
God comfort you in the shadow of death
Give us this day, our daily bread
And prayers for you
I said, I said

Up the rutted lane the post-man came
Worn sombre face and cycle-clips
In his hand the yellow telegram
And time stood still while my heart raced
Numbed with grief – no tears to shed
"A reply?" – "No reply"
I said, I said

And so the start of my beige coloured days
The greyness of torment in years to come
No surrendered virginity – no bright horizon
I cry for children I would have borne
I weep for the life we could have led
"I'll wait for you"
I said, I said

BRAZIL 2016

In Brazil there are Brazilians
Picking coffee beans in zillions
And footballers earn millions
Kicking balls
In the Amazonian River
Snakes and caiman slither
From Iguazu waters quiver
Over falls

Tarantulas stalk and wander
Tripping over anaconda
And the sloths will stop and ponder
Run a mile
Join the carnival in Rio
And sing and dance and limbo
With Senhoritas – arms akimbo
Latin style

We can party with maracas
Let off the old fire crackers
If they think that they can whack us
At the Games
We'll send sons and sporty daughters
Across Atlantic waters
With their fans and their supporters
Raise the flame

In gear from Marks & Spencer
We'll send them our best fencer
Which no-one there will censor
Or deport
They can swim and run and cycle
In lycra from St. Michael
The Olympian disciple
God of Sport

With England's finest gymnasts bold
All awarded medals Gold
Their picture on the centre-fold
It's written
Olympic athletes at their peak
The greatest sportsmen since the Greek
Showing skills and their technique
For Britain

BRUSH WITH CARE

When you go on vacation
The destination you can choose
But you meet the nice and nasty
On a transatlantic cruise

In the cabin next to ours
This Yankee-Doodle pair
She was all of six feet wide
And he grew nostril hair

We had this lovely steward
A Filipino lad
He cleaned and tidied for us
But they treated him real bad

They were loud and rude and flashy
And they spoke to him like dirt
Never stopping to consider
The vulnerable can be hurt

This boy could not retaliate
And before I could think twice
With a little whisper in his ear
I gave him this advice

"When you clean their bathroom
Before the toilet flushes
Give the bowl a good scrub round
Using their tooth-brushes"

Yes, I know that it's disgusting
But I said it tongue in cheek
To cheer up this unhappy lad
Long suffering and meek

Honest, I was joking
Please don't let it be said
That I was complicit with
Putting ideas in his head

But I caught the eye of our attendant
He gave a secret smile of thanks
'Though not a word was spoken
He'd got even with those Yanks

BRUTAL FREEDOM

The tourists keep on coming
They stand there gawping at
Plastic models of the railway bridge
And other tourist tat

But rarely will they question
No lone voice asking why
So many young men perished
To build the bridge across the Kwai

They've read the book and seen the film's
Dramatic history
But as they lick their ice-creams
Will they spare a thought for me

They enjoy their life of freedom
These women and their men
They'll never have the understanding
Of how it was back then

The day that starts before the sun
Has kissed this luscious land
Just a scoop of scummy water
Drunk from a calloused hand

Our gang of guards in sweat-stained shirts
Wave bayonet and gun
These little men with almond eyes
They count us – one by one

This enemy does not respect
The Convention of Geneva
Twenty more have died this night
From dysentery and fever

Now we weak and starved must stumble
Broken spirit, aching back
To hack a path-way through the jungle
For the Siam to Burma track

A few grams of rice with maggots
From captors so depraved
For every sleeper on the railway track
A man goes to his grave

Years of torture and brutality
Forty-three to forty-five
Thirteen hundred POW's
And a hundred thousand natives died

Now calm and peace enfold me
Lying sodden in the rain
No longer does my body feel
The whipped and beaten pain

I dream of you and England
And embrace with dying breath
No more to fear tomorrow
For my freedom is my death

CHRISTMAS AT MINE

Way back in the summer
In the garden, fuelled with Pimms
Topped up with flutes of Champers
And a tonic with three gins

In a spirit of benevolence
And full of bonhomie
I asked all my relations
To spend Christmas Day with me

There's a problem with the numbers
Thirteen did I invite
With just a table and six chairs
The seating will be tight

First a small Amontillado
A medicinal little drink
To evoke the Christmas spirit
Help with thoughts I've got to think

I've looked up on the internet
A recipe by Mary Berry
But it all looks complicated
So I'll need another sherry

There's Festive Fare – a glossy mag
Could that come to my aid
I bought some figs in brandy
But I drank the marinade

I've called upon Nigella
A dish that's hall-marked 'Lawson'
But my efforts just resemble
Piano playing by Les Dawson

Now they're on their way for Christmas
And I'm going to write a list
Of everything essential
So that nothing will be missed

I've already got a headache
I don't think I can hack it
I'd better get some *pince mies*
Lidl's, fifty pence a packet

On Christmas Eve – a *dishy fish*
So *coin of lod* is what I need
With *motatoes* and *asgarapus*
Crusted with *waycara* seed

An extra *vabletege* could be
Librocco cooked al dente
With *ninted mew topatoes*
And *snippars* served a-plenty

Some nice flowers for a *pentre-ciece*
Sarniscus I could pick
Along with *dendorhodrons*
And some leaves of *moreasyc*

How about some bronze *chrymumsanthems*
Buby raubles – I'll buy three
And lots of *wintkling sintel*
I can drape around the tree

With *Sprussel Brouts* and *chutnest* stuffing
On Christmas Day a *kurtey* roast
Lipochatas, bigs in plankets
And some *stead bricks* made of toast

I'll buy a nice big *chox of boxlates*
With *molly* and some *histletoe*
Some *chaper-pains* for *recordation*
And some *fartiticial* snow

So now my list is written
I deserve another sherry
It's the fifth I've had this morning
'Tis the season to be merry

(Work out the inebriated anagrams)

COMPUTER GAMES

The telephone is ringing
I jump up and shake my head
It's only seven-thirty
And I'm sound asleep in bed

It must be some emergency
With trepidation say "Hello"
And a foreign voice informs me
"Your computer's going slow"

He asks "How are you today?"
Says his name is John or Paul
But sounds just like the chappie
Serving curry in Bengal

I know that he's a scammer
And I'm filled with red-hot rage
I guess I'm on his 'Suckers List'
Made vulnerable with age

But my wits are not yet addled
And now he's on the line
I'll teach him a lesson
Play along and waste his time

So I tell him how I'm feeling
With arthritis in my knees
And problems with my water-words
Each time I cough or sneeze

To control my computer
Is the reason that he dials
But I'll tell him of my visit
To the Doctor, with my piles

My ankles are all swollen
I've a bunion on my toe
It's not just my computer
On the blink and going slow

I ask him to shout louder
But I'm trying not to laugh
As he bellows down the telephone
I'm neither deaf nor daft

He says fixing my computer
Is his one and only aim
Yeah – right – you scheming scum-bag
Let's get on a play your game

I tell him my computer
Is on the floor below
And would he kindly hold on
While down the stairs I slowly go

I watch the clock and make some tea
And when I think I've reached his limit
I wheeze and say "I'm nearly there
Just wait another minute"

He's sure that he has got me
My computer to control
To infiltrate my software
Oh – the poor deluded soul

He thinks I'm sat before the screen
And nothing can go wrong
But then I sweetly ask him
"How do I switch it on?"

I flap and fiddle round a while
And agree with him, it's slow
But say "The screen's now lit up
So let's give it a go"

He says "Now press the Windows key"
I understand alright
But say "I'm sitting by the window
And getting lots of light"

He's getting agitated
Says "Find the key with coloured square"
So I tell him that I've found it
To stop him tearing out his hair

Now I explain I've got rheumatics
And my fingers are all numb
And would he please be patient
As I type slowly with my thumb

Still we're clocking up the time
I'll keep him on his toes
"Hang on a minute, petal
Now I have to blow my nose"

He instructs me then to type an 'R'
I ask "Is that 'A'-'R'-'E'
In upper-case or lower-case?"
And "Where do I find the key?"

He says type 'R' for Romeo
I say "That's Shakespeare, pet"
And ask him very nicely
"Please can I type Juliette?"

Pretending then to hold the 'R'
Ask "Is that what you mean?
'Cos now I've got a million 'R's
Spread right across the screen"

I quite enjoy a challenge
I laugh 'til I'm in tears
And this nasty little scammer
Has steam coming out his ears

These calls brighten up my day
How quickly the time passes
I ask him now to "Hang on, dear"
Because I've lost my glasses

All this time we're talking
And he hasn't cottoned on
I'm not at the computer
So nothing can go wrong

So while I've got my marbles
Astute and still alert
I keep the scammers talking
To stop others getting hurt

When I'm bored with playing
And all's been done and said
I explain the nurse has just arrived
To put me back to bed

DEAD OR ALIVE

Have you ever been on Amazon
The company – not the river
Where you order stuff on line
And next day they deliver?

There's adverts in all languages
French, Russian, Chinese too
And an Eskimo could order
Shivering in his ice igloo

So when I wrote my little book
And gave it them to sell
I liked their advertising blurb
And the picture turned out well.

And then I saw the small print
And threw a fit at what I read
They said 'The author of this book
Is deceased – and she is dead'

They said I was key witness
Of events that fateful day
To the murder of a President
In Dallas, U.S.A.

It said I was a teacher
And when Kennedy was shot
I was standing there alongside
And I saw the blooming lot

How can they have it all so wrong?
Another Jean Hill who's a writer
I pinch myself; no, I'm not dead
So that makes me feel brighter

Then I text this guy called Rahman
On the Customer Service line
Thinking he could fix things
And all would turn out fine

The text read like a film scrip
A comedy at that
He didn't speak much English
Not much help and that's a fact

So he got someone to 'phone me
His accent was Chinese
I said "You've got the author wrong
Will you correct it, please"

He didn't understand me
No answer could he give
By now it's nearly mid-night
And I've lost the will to live

I told him I was still alive
Assured him and I said
"Listen to me breathing
Can you hear me? I'm not dead"

So now I've emailed details
All the poems are by me
And I'm still alive and kicking
Even though I'm seventy-three

I'm not the famous Jean Hill
Who gained notoriety that day
When Oswald shot the President
And Kennedy passed away

I'm just Jean Hill from England
And I write poetry – a lot
Although I'm no Spring Chicken
Not ready for the cooking pot

I haven't any claim to fame
A lowly writer and a poet
Please Amazon sort your data-base
If I were dead I'd know it!

This is unbelievable but true

DEPRESSION

(ACROSTIC)

Deep despair, blacker than the blackest night

Enveloping darkness, no glimmer of light

Pointless existence, with no will to thrive

Relentless fatigue, more dead than alive

Exhaustion that's mental, so nobody knows

Silent, oppressive, anxiety grows

Self-harm, mutilate, thoughts torture a brain

Inflict and destroy, there's feeling in pain

Others who've been there, perhaps recognise

Negative feelings, when a mind quietly dies

DRIVEL

I'm at the peak of my verbosity
The poems keep on flowing
The ink's run out my biro
And the computer screen is glowing

I'm not a poet of distinction
And I've not got much potential
But I'll keep on with this drivel
'Til the lead runs out my pencil

ESCAPE

I've woken up again today
Every morning it's the same
I wish things could be different
Escape the meaningless mundane

Sometimes I wake up grumpy
Pull the curtains – see grey sky
Another day to get through
As the long hours multiply

What could I do that's different?
To bring meaning to my life
Or will be written my headstone
'Here lies a good housewife'

I think I'll be a nudist
Enjoy freedom and fresh air
It could be the real solution
Since I've not a thing to wear

The wardrobe may be chock-a-block
But nothing in there fits
Would all the other nudists
Overlook my wobbly bits

But I think I'd have to diet
Look good – slimmed to the bone
But another problem haunts me
Where do nudists keep their 'phone?

FLAMING FIASCO

We've got brand new neighbours
Gwendoline and Frank
She's a local magistrate
And he's manager of the bank

Well, thinking we should meet them
We thought it would be fun
If we held a garden barbecue
And invited them to come

I bought some steak and canapes
And foil wrapped rainbow trout
So when everything was ready
Across the fence we gave a shout

I extended a warm welcome
A party spirit to infuse
With a little sausage on a stick
And a glass of home-made booze

I guess we looked quite casual
In shorts and old sun-hat
Gwendoline wore a cardigan
And Frank had a cravat

With eyebrows raised a fraction
Her grey hair tightly permed
But to make a good impression
I'd left no stone unturned

Time to light the barbeque
My husband struck a match
Even though he struck a box full
The darn thing wouldn't catch

We threw on lighter fluid
And a can of paraffin
A little dash of petrol
And some nitro-glycerine

To make sure that it lit up
We applied the old blow-torch
It went up like a rocket
And set fire to their porch

The spread of flames was rapid
With smoke yellow and dense
And though I called the fire-brigade
It soon engulfed their fence

Gwendoline had hysterics
And furious was Frank
You don't expect that language
From the manager of a bank

With greenhouse glass all shattered
Their conifers lost in flame
I think it was at this point
That I knew we'd get the blame

It roared up their pagoda
The conservatory copped it too
And through it all blazed merrily
Our flaming barbecue

Now Gwen and Frank don't speak to us
With their home annihilated
And I've come to the conclusion
That barbecues are over-rated

FROM PERTH TO ADELAIDE

I saw the advert in the paper
For The Wanderer of the Sea
To cruise around Australia
And thought 'Wow' that's for me

So via Kuala Lumpur
I went without a blip
And waiting there 'down under'
Was my gigantic ship

The best thing about cruising
You get off the boat each day
And visit all the places that
You pass along the way

To start our epic journey
From Perth to Adelaide
A thousand miles all nautical
Three days on board I stayed

Well, trapped on this great liner
The Wanderer of the Ocean
I grabbed myself a deck-chair
And slapped on sun-tan lotion

I gazed at the horizon
But the scene remained the same
So I signed up for some classes
To exercise my brain

At the ship's cocktail party
Photos taken with the captain
Then next day morning classes
Fifty ways to fold a napkin

There's mini-golf and mountaineering
And on the adult climbing wall
O.A.P's strapped with elastic
Making sure that they don't fall

There's fun for every age group
And to encourage gender mixes
They've got nude trampolining
'Specially for the over sixties

Each night I'd join the disco
And I gave it my best shot
I'd jerk around like puppets
With my strings tied in a knot

There's so much entertainment
You can learn another lingo
Or take up 'toss the bean bag'
Table-tennis or play bingo

You can have your body pummelled
With gunge to detoxify
But I'd rather spend the morning
Sticking pins into my eye

You can decorate a cupcake
Or do some origami
Or run round and round the deck track
Like a hamster going barmy

There's bungy jumping for the fittest
And if pensioners complain
They strap them in a harness
With a bouncing Zimmer frame

But come the dusk and twilight
Each evening it gets better
In luxury I'd dine in style
Then go off to the theatre

There's lots of fellow cruisers
So you can take your pick
From the bright and intellectual
To pug-ugly and the thick

With champagne cocktails flowing
'Neath sparkling chandeliers
Gentlemen in black ties
Wives with diamond studded ears

With delicacies of distinction
All served with great panache
And for those with caps on back-to-front
There's beer and pie and mash

For those who can't be bothered
To dress – it's for the best
They go to the self-service
In flip-flops and string vest

The crew and the attendants
Work hard with smiling faces
But sadly not all passengers
Are blessed with social graces

Three days incarceration
But I've nearly got it made
For on the great horizon
Are the shores of Adelaide

FROM URCHIN TO ANAHEIM

Hear the bell of Big Ben chime
As here I sit in London's grime
With blackened face, you'll see that I'm
An urchin raised to a life of crime

Oh, Yankee fella, in your prime
Throw me a nickel, dollar or dime
Let me dream of a life sublime
In a land of plenty, lemons and lime

There is no reason, nor any rhyme
To halt my longings, impede my climb
To raise myself from the muck and slime
And grant me a life in the summer-time

HUBBLE BUBBLE TROUBLE

The thirty-first October
Is the best day in the life
Of Wizard Ernie Has-Bean
And Enid, Has-Bean's wife

Ernie flames the cauldron
Enid chants the 'Sin of Sloth'
They stir it up together
And concoct a noxious broth

With scale of fish and hair of hen
And glossy hornets' wing
With the stew a-bubbly-popping
Enid adds a dash of gin

Then Enid serves up dinner
And Ernie takes a slurp
Says it gives him indigestion
And to prove it gives a burp

So Wizard Ernie Has-Bean
Rings up his friends and seers
Says "I'm sick of cauldron muck
Let's meet up for some beers"

But Enid waved her witches wand
And with her dander fired
Shoved Ernie in the cauldron
Where he gurgled and expired

Then Enid charged her SatNav
Put the lid on old Has-Bean
And flying on her broomstick
Celebrated Halloween

IT'S 'AULD LANG SYNE' FOR HENRY

(*A Discipline in Rhyme*)

Henry was a 'dandy'
Superior, rich and *fine*
Slim of hip but slack of jaw
And nose quite *aquiline*

He took his favourite girl-friend
The noble *Adeline*
Rowing in a rowing boat
Of gleaming varnished *pine*

Across the park and on the waters
Of the rippling *Serpentine*
He had erotic visions where
Their limbs would all *entwine*

Eating canapés and caviar
And sipping sparkling *wine*
And how her eyes would flutter
And on him with brilliance *shine*

He'd hand-feed her black grapes
From his pater's hot-house *vine*
And take box at Ascot
To race and bet on the *equine*

But the one thing Henry lacked
Was back-bone, spunk and *spine*
When dressed up in his finery
He took her out to *dine*

A quick caress – one little kiss
Saw he'd over-stepped the *line*
With a hard left-hook she floored him
It surely was a *sign*

And with Henry seeing stars she said
"You are no beau of *mine*"
It's sad that I can't be *benign*
And your character now *malign*

For your amorous advances
I must hasten to *decline*
You're a prat, a brat, an imbecile
And you're quite *asinine*

I could never be your true love
Your wife or *concubine*
I'd rather live in a council flat
With your mate *Frankenstein*"

Then she gave a mighty shove
Pushed him in the swirling *brine*
Nobody could save him
'Though they dabbed on *Calamine*

So they pickled his soaked torso
In a cask of *Turpentine*
And on his tombstone in the grave-yard
A veritable *shrine* ……

*'Here lies the body of dear Henry
Aristocrat and Swine!'*

LITTER-PICKER'S LAMENT

I'm a pillar of society
I'd not set out to fight
When I had this altercation
In the pub on Saturday night

Let me explain the situation
The predicament I'm in
Circumstance will then absolve me
From the stain of any sin …..

I'm ashamed to see the litter
Adorning every city street
And the worst is left by smokers
Outside places where we eat

So I rang the local council
And when we spoke on the 'phone
I gave them quite an earful
As they listened to me moan

I complained about the debris
The mess that we walk through
And then I asked quite curtly
Just what they planned to do.

They said they had a little gang
Of helpful volunteers
Who picked up litter on a Sunday
And would that allay my fears

So I found myself recruited
To this 'do-gooding' group
The council gave me plastic bags
A shovel and a scoop

They sent a load of rubber gloves
A peaked cap in a packet
And in a lovely shade of yellow
A fluorescent jacket

Along with full instructions
Came a stick with handy claw
For picking up the rubbish
That the yobs drop on the floor

I must be polite at all times
To the public I might see
So tongue in cheek and bare-faced
I ticked the box that said 'Agree'

Well-armed with my equipment
'Job's Worth' cap and keen ambition
I set about to clean the streets
A litter-picker on a mission

The reward for my endeavour
Was pavements all pristine
No crisp packets or beer cans
Or pizza boxes to be seen

Then as 'clean street' vigilante
Showed no mercy – no excuse
I put my new equipment
To a much better use

This lout stood propping up the bar
And breaking every law
Was chucking all his fag-ends
Out the Nag's Head front door

So I nabbed this litter-dropper
Cap back-to-front and thick
And opened up the claw-like end
And whacked him with my stick

But then it wasn't my fault
The claw-end wouldn't close
And it did a lot of damage
When I shoved it up his nose

His mate who tried to intervene
A spotty nincompoop
I smacked him with my shovel
And my doggy pooper-scoop

The drinkers at the bar joined in
And half of them were sloshed
And in the furore that ensued
My council hat got squashed

They ripped the logo off my jacket
A garment that I'd cherished
What really made me lose my rag
My rubbers gloves had perished

So I had to face the magistrate
Charged with 'Battery and Intent'
And he asked if I was sorry
Yes, I was – my stick got bent

Then they threw in for good measure
My sentence to increase
'Incitement to Cause Riot'
And 'Disturber of the Peace'

And if that wasn't bad enough
To add insult to injury
He fined me for the misuse
Of council property

….. So now you know my story
Does my punishment fit the crime
With my dustcart and my shovel
Sweeping up the roadside grime

To do Community Service
And a lifetime on probation
Picking up the litter for
The local corporation

LONG SWIM

I like a nice fresh sandwich
With prawns stuffed in the middle
So I wrote myself a shopping list
And off I went to Lidl

I found them high upon a shelf
Can't believe how far they'd swam
Clearly written on the label
Said they'd come from Vietnam

These prawns so pink and tasty
Braved the tempest of the sea
To be frozen in a packet
And de-frosted for my tea

MAN OR MOUSE

Isn't science wonderful
The drug controller NICE
Has authorised the research
To restore hearing to deaf mice

So they took some little mouses
And peered in each furry ear
And fed them pills and potions
To help the deaf mice hear

The trials were quite successful
And the mice now circumvented
They're trying out on humans
The treatment they've invented

Well, being hard of hearing
I thought it would be great
That in this research project
I could participate

But it's had its side effects
Now when I try to speak
The most that I can manage is
A rather timid squeak

I looked into the mirror
And gave myself a fright
Instead of manly stubble
I'd grown whiskers overnight

They said the pills had side-effects
From the chemist where I got 'em
But now, quite long and hairy
A tail grows out my bottom

Though my ears are getting better
The sound's no longer foggy
But every time I venture out
I'm chased by next-door's moggie

And now my wife has left me
Saying 'Are you Man or Mouse?'
She trapped me in the garden shed
And banned me from the house

So now I've got a new wife
And I gave her paw a squeeze
With a quick twitch of my whiskers
I said "Minnie, pass the cheese"

What I want to know is – Where did they find all the deaf mice?

MODEL POET

I'm a writer and a speaker
Of poems that provoke
But most of it is funny stuff
A verse, a rhyme, a joke

So on a wet and windy night
In answer to a call
I prepared my presentation
And set off to find the hall

After driving through the tempest
I found the place alright
And dashed into the entrance
A soaked dishevelled sight

I thought I was quite early
And could dry off in the loo
But a hand reached out and grabbed me
"You're late, quick, come on through"

The chap in charge stepped forward
Said "You're not what we expected
We ordered from the agency
And you're not who we selected"

"But beggars can't be choosers"
He eyed me with a frown
And asked how I'd prefer it
Sitting up or laying down

He said for preparation
I could go behind the screen
I said "I'd rather stand here
Where I'll be heard and seen"

He said "Well, get your kit off
Let's get on and make a start
To paint you in your birthday suit
Will challenge any art"

"You're no longer in the first flush
Of youth and style and vigour
To be an artists' model
You should have a firmer figure"

He waved me to the sofa
"We'll not pay the going rate
We wanted someone nubile
Not past their sell-by-date"

They all stared at me quizzically
Their look, in fact, quite rude
If they thought that I'd read poetry
Stood before them in the nude

With dander up but ego flattened
I said "Let me elucidate
I don't fill *your* requirements
But at Poetry – I'm great!"

"I don't want to be your pin-up
I'm leaving now, it's for the best
You don't want to paint a model
Who wears a thermal vest"

"I'm here as a guest-speaker
Of poems, verse and rhyme
I've got the date and place right
But arrived at the wrong time"

I retreated to the car park
And realised my mistake
Art Class starts at seven
And Poetry's half-past eight

MY RED BUS

When I was a little girl
Aged just three or four
My Mum bought me a red bus
Which I raced around the floor

Made of tin with gears and wheels
And nuts and bolts and sprocket
It whizzed and whirled with cogs and coils
Across the lino like a rocket

We'd never heard of Health & Safety
And with no cover there to hide
Were all the inner workings
Flying round and round inside

Well, one afternoon in winter
As the fire burned warm and bright
I turned the key of my red bus
And wound it up real tight

I climbed upon a little stool
And as Dad dozed in his chair
I lifted up my clockwork bus
And placed it on his hair

The cogs and wheels spun madly
And with an anguished scream
His hair wrapped round the sprockets
Leaving scalp where hair had been

He yelled and leapt around the room
My red bus on his head
The cogs and gears still spinning
Was there blood – oh yes – he bled

He pulled and tugged and twisted
But still the wheels rotated
Mum tried to find the scissors
But they couldn't be located

So she grabbed his cut-throat razor
And with a frantic yelp
Sliced across his hair-line
And hacked it off his scalp

Sad to say I got the blame
That amid his scars and scratches
He became aged prematurely
But his hair grew back – in patches

I cried and said "I'm sorry"
The fact was hard to bear
My red toy bus stopped working
It was all clogged up with hair

True story circa 1947

ONE-ARMED BEAR

The city gent was passing
The workhouse door that night
His heart was wrenched with pity
For the poor and their sad plight

To the child crouched on the cobbles
He asked "Why sit here on your own"
With a shy smile she responded
"Kind Sir, I'm not alone"

She showed him then her Peggy-Doll
And wooden horse curled in her palm
And hugging to her tightly
A teddy-bear with just one arm

"I've not known a father
But my mother rests above
She went to heaven with our new born
But still protects me with her love"

"I hear my mother's soft voice
In the rustling of the trees
I feel her kiss upon my cheek
In each fanning of the breeze"

"I hear her happy laughter
In the bubbling of the streams
And every night I share with her
The sweetness of my dreams"

The humbled gent went on his way
But not wanting to forsake her
To bring some brightness in her life
He called the town's toy-maker

"Carve the finest rocking horse
With leather reins and flying mane
And make a doll with golden hair
And a face of porcelain"

"Dress the doll in lace and silk
With petticoats to wear
And stitch and stuff a panda
To replace that one-armed bear"

The child shook her head sadly
"Dear Sir, these toys I can't accept
To exchange gifts Mother gave me"
And she smiled her sweet regrets

"Give to those less fortunate
I have my own dear family
Peg-Doll, Horse and One-Armed Bear
And my mother's memory"

So the gent asked the toymaker
"A simple job – a small repair
Please stitch and craft a matching arm
For a well-loved one-armed bear"

OUR JERUSALEM

What's happened to the twin-set
And discreet string of pearls
The back-bone of old England
With tight-permed blue-rinsed curls

The anchor of society
The Institutes and Guilds
The Summer Fete and Garden Party
In England's jewel-green fields

Let's stand up for our values
While politicians chew the cud
And plunge this brave and sovereign isle
Into a sea of third-world mud

Wave the banner of tradition
In this land where we abide
Fight adversity with valour
And fly the flag with pride

POLITICAL CONES

I'm driving up to London
Nose to tail on the M4
With road-works at each junction
And traffic cones galore

There's miles of red and white ones
As the drivers they direct
And some of different colours
All politically correct

The blue cones – they are Tory
Struggling up a steep incline
Trying hard to find the right route
But present a thin blue line

There are blue ones of distinction
A yellow band around the cones
Are they Lib-Dem Alliance
With Tory overtones

There lurking in the hedgerow
And sometimes never seen
Are the cones of verdant colour
For the party of The Green

But running red and rampant
Are cones of Labour hue
I've side-swiped quite a lot of them
And tried to squash a few

But with political correctness
To ensure we come full circle
Let's get in touch with UKIP
We need some cones in purple

But I'm keeping my eyes open
For shades of bully-blue
And they'd have stars around them
Representing the EU

So let's get on with Brexit
Make sure the day won't come
When we have blue and starry cones
Lined up on the M1

RARE TREAT

Dan-Dan – a missionary man
For his wife, Di, had a plan
In exchange for fire-water
The cannibals caught her
And they all had a rare Steak Diane

RICHES FOR MARIGOLD

The streets of London, so I'm told
Are shining bright, all paved with gold
So young and old, leave house and fold
They are a wonder to behold

For riches, the Devil your soul be sold
To seek your fortune, brave sleet and cold
Stride out brave hearts, be fearless, bold
Make haste, a new life's there to mould

Soon with servants all to scold
Mistress of her own household
A celebrity on the centrefold
I'll give to my wife, Marigold

ROCK 'n ROLL YEARS

Hold my hand and sit beside me
Drink your cocoa while it's hot
We were young and carefree once
Before we 'tied the knot'

You had just turned seventeen
D.A. haircut slicked with grease
And I followed in your foot-steps
Thought those days would never cease

At The Palais down in Hammersmith
We'd dance 'til light of day
You'd buy me a Babycham
And we'd twist the night away

We'd bop to Elvis Presley
And jive to Jailhouse Rock
And with the music of Bill Hayley
We'd Rock Around the Clock

I would pose and prance and pout
And your stance mean and moody
You were true King of the Teds
And you called me your 'Judy'

With velvet collar, jacket draped
A bootlace was your tie
And I swished my long ponytail
Or beehive style combed high

I dipped my head in peroxide
Mother went quite mad
Although my hair resembled straw
The colour wasn't bad

I remember well my rolled up jeans
And circle skirt with polka dots
But way back in the fifties
It was the blokes who called the shots

We lived throughout the 'cold-war'
Ban the Bomb was all the news
And you wore drainpipe trousers
And crepe-soled blue suede shoes

In the back of your Dad's Zephyr
We enhanced our carnal knowledge
Sex had been invented
We did Biology in college

We might not remember yesterday
As life's moments we enjoy
Here beside you – I'm your 'Judy'
And you're still my Teddy Boy

So hold your cocoa steady love
Take a sip before it's cold
I wouldn't want to change our life
As together we've grown old

We'd never tell the children
They'd not believe the truth
But we'll reminisce the fifties
And re-live our misspent youth

The duck's ass is a haircut style that was popular during the 1950s, or simply D.A., and is also described as slicked back hair. Teddy Boys girlfriends were Teddy Girls, also known as Judies

ROCKING THE BOAT

From the time of Boadicea
To Thatcher, Merkel, May
Through the corridors of power
These women paved the way

Suffragettes rocked many boats
And generations of their daughters
Have pushed aside the barriers
To swim male infested waters

In the world of banking
We have girly 'city slickers'
And in the Church of England
We have lovely female vicars

And now we have appointed
Stockport's Bishop, Libby Lane
To this role of high achievement
The first woman to ordain

We've yet to take the next step
But we live in futile hope
That one day in the Vatican
We'll have a lady Pope

And it may be a cliché
But we have always known
The hand that rocks the cradle
Is the power behind the throne

SAVAGED

We went on an excursion
My other half and me
To local parks and gardens
And a wild-bird sanctuary

We wandered round the cages
With not much else to do
Until we saw a sign that said
'Come and Feed the Cockatoo'

So with camera at the ready
We found the man who sold it
And bought a dish of birdseed
And my husband said he'd hold it

We entered the enclosure
Of the great white cockatoo
And hubby held the seed bowl out
As he'd been told to do

It was then the trouble started
Those huge winged birds took flight
With my loved one in the middle
Of a claw and feather fight

With talons sharp as daggers
They tore through hair and skin
And although he fought them bravely
With these birds he couldn't win

I took some quite nice photos
They're predominately red
You can't see him for feathers
And all the blood he shed

We didn't think these crested birds
Could do him so much harm
His head's got criss-cross claw marks
And chunks gouged out his arm

He's one ear looking tattered
Where the birds have pecked it
The attendant sympathetic
As he dabbed on antiseptic

We hurried off to A & E
For tetanus injections
And strong antibiotics
To ward off bird infections

But now he's got this problem
Disturbed by a neurosis
He thinks he's growing feathers
And developed psittacosis

And one thing more I'll tell you
He thinks I haven't noticed
A pointy sharp and yellow beak
Replaces his proboscis

Because of our excursion
He's now got avian flu
And I'm seeing our solicitor
To ask if we can sue

I'm seeking compensation
Some insurance money too
And on the claim I've written
'Savaged by a cockatoo'

Based on truth but dramatized!
It happened in Australia

SWITCH IT OFF

Some producers on the telly
Make programs that offend
With 'F' words and the sex scenes
As rules of decency they bend

Between whatever gender
Flash graphic sexual scenes
Do we really want this
On our television screens

Do they set out to shock us
With every view more crude
With bodies in the bedroom
Writhing in the nude

Well, I glance at my husband
And with a discreet little cough
Reaching out for the remote
We switch the darn thing off

TEN COMMANDMENTS

Dear Lord, life's a struggle
Your commandments so to keep
Sticking to the straight and narrow
Day by day and week by week
So would it be so awful
To make me a millionaire
So life's trials and tribulations
Would be easier to bear

I've gone forth just like you told me
Multiplied and given birth
But in case I don't make heaven
Please reward me here on earth
Now grant me your indulgence
Just in case you haven't seen
For I know that you'll reward me
When you read how good I've been

I promise I've not worshipped
Other Gods – but can you see
There's this pompous boss at work
Who lords it over me
He's got a self-made halo
That illuminates his head
And, alongside you God
Has the power to strike me dead

I steer clear of graven images
Don't bow to wealth and fame
But if I grovel for a pay rise
The circumstances you should blame
I won't worship other idols
But I ask with trepidation
Don't visit sins that I commit
On a future generation

When I'm at the cash machine
I don't take your name in vain
When the screen displayed before me says
'You're in the red again'
I might say 'Gawd' and 'Blimey'
And rant and swear a bit
The old man's on the dole this week
'Cos he's a lazy git

I've no trouble with the Sabbath
To break this commandment is a sin
And with your blessing dear Lord God
I'll have a nice lie-in
My husband's drowning sorrows
But he'll want his dinner soon
The boozer shuts at half-past three
But I'll stay in bed 'til noon

I'd honour both my mother
And my father or my sire
But it could be one of many
From the local male voice choir
She spread her favours widely
Had an eye that liked to roam
Now she entertains the gentlemen
In a geriatric home

I've not committed murder
Though my husband isn't thrilled
Because I'm menopausal
He could be kissed or killed
And still on the same subject Lord
The bit 'Thou shalt not kill'
I'm just OK unless you count
The contraceptive pill

When it comes to adultery
I'll try not to come a cropper
But I love a man in uniform
And I've met this hunky copper
His whistle and his truncheon
Put my virtue in a muddle
We had a secret rendezvous
Behind the bike-shed for a cuddle

When you ask me not to steal
Well, perhaps I'm somewhat lax
Will you overlook the little fiddle
Of my annual income tax
I need to earn some extra
To moonlight on the side
I never seems to make ends meet
And, God, you know I've tried

Will I bear false witness
Just a little sin you'd find
I bunged up the parking meter
And I blamed the bloke behind
Can we forget insurance claims
I needed extra cash
It was just a dented bumper
When they paid out for whip-lash

I promise I won't covet
My neighbour's ass or ox
But I'd quite like their telly
A fifty-four inch goggle-box
But I don't fancy her husband
He's a dopey sod like mine
And they only drive a Skoda
So that commandment's fine

I've kept most of your rulings
I've said my prayers each night
To be rich wouldn't spoil me
And with heavenly foresight
Please let me win the lottery
Lots of cash – a huge amount
And I'll invest it wisely
In a nice Swiss bank account

So I gaze into your heaven God
See the moon and sky so starry
And would it be too much to ask
For a brand new red Ferrari
A small yacht in the Bahamas
Or just give me half a chance
To buy myself a chateau
Somewhere in the South of France

I'd like a Tiffany tiara
Sparkling diamonds, drops of pearl
A designer gown in midnight lace
In which to twist and twirl
And God, I need a face-lift
Will you pay for liposuction
Or a nice cosmetic surgeon
And a two-stone weight reduction

If I've committed misdemeanours
Dear God, I'd make amends
If only you would buy me
A new Mercedes Benz
I'd like to drive a Bentley
But what I want the most
Is drive a Rolls Royce to the Ritz
And say 'Park the Silver Ghost'

To see me sitting in my pinny
That can't be your grand design
When I've kept your ten commandments
And toed the flaming line
I think you overlooked me
As I drew the shortest straw
Please could you re-arrange things
So that I end up with more

I know I've not been perfect
Created in your image true
But will you consider carefully
This missive sent to you
If the meekest will inherit
Send a sign and tell me how
They'll get their reward in heaven
But, dear God, I want mine now

THE FORGOTTEN SOLDIER

Remember well the famous line
'Age Shall Not Weary Them'
Of heroes now forgotten
In the century since then

I can't claim to be a hero
But I served my country true
And in the words of Churchill
'So many owed so few'

I still hear echoes of the past
The parade, the pomp, the glory
The marching of survivors
Who came home to tell their story

The passing years – they've wearied me
Now with unsteady gait
Facing empty isolation
A discharged soldier's fate

In a damp and lonely bed-sit
Through a grimy window pane
With curled and peeling paintwork
On a rotting window frame

A wall, a yard, so grey and bare
No ray of sun to cheer
Just a stretch of cracking concrete
Unchanging through the year

My friends, the London pigeons
With their mangled city feet
Wait coldly on the window sill
As each dawn I sadly greet

Oh, grey birds with your pearlized breast
Feed from this hand extended
And with your cooing grant me solace
'Til this old soldier's life is ended

THE MINER'S LAD

"Hold the lantern higher, lad
Light the path we have to go
The track is rough and stony
And the ruts are filled with snow

Do not tarry now, me boyo
Two more miles – we can't be late
Hear the parish clock a-chiming
Soon they'll close the pit-head gate

Today you'll be a man, my son
But for you I wanted better
You've learnt to sum and reckon
Read a book and write a letter

But now my lad, my first-born
Your future's down the mine
You had twelve years of childhood
I was hewing coal aged nine

Your Ma, she's done us proud, son
And although your back will ache
We've bread and dripping in our snap tins
And a lump of lardy-cake

Today I'll walk beside you
Soon you'll tread this path alone
Take good care of your mother, boy
There's five mouths to feed back home

So hold the lantern higher, lad
There's still a mile to go"
And the miner coughed and spat his spit
Streaked crimson in the snow

THE PHOTOGRAPH

When we say Good-Bye and leave you
When our time on earth is through
Don't think of us as 'oldies'
Remember we were young once too

When you open up the album
And you see the photographs
Each one there a memory
Of joy and tears and laughs

See me here at seventeen
And Dad just twenty-two
Starting life together
A fragile love that grew

Maturing years when you were born
And nurtured with our care
A story told in pictures
Each and every photo there

So with our ashes scattered
Beneath The Ridges tree
Walk that pathway sometimes
And remember Dad and me

THE WEIGHTY WITCH

Hi – Lucinda Lug-Worm calling
On witches wave-length – one, two, three
I've trouble with my broomstick
Please can the AA assist me?

With a shudder, jolt and judder
The broomstick took a dive
Now here I am hitch-hiking
Up the M-twenty-five

The nice AA Patrolman
Said he'd give it a try
But when I sat down upon it
The thing refused to fly

And so I took my broomstick
To the garage up the road
With shaking head they sighed and said
"It can't carry such a load"

I used to be a thin witch
A skinny, scrawny crone
But with all that Trick and Treating
I now weigh twenty-stone

They re-set all the bristles
And they used the strongest twine
But these new slim-line broomsticks
Won't carry bottoms such as mine

Now I sit lonely by the cauldron
Alongside my green-eyed cat
I've taken out my dentures
And put aside my witches hat

And I'm tipping out the stew-pot
No more witches brew cuisine
With just lettuce and Ryvita
It's a blooming awful Halloween

TOO LATE MR. BUTTERWORTH

I'm in love with Nigel Butterworth
But he looks down his nose at me
He's a big-wig on the council
And I'm the one who makes the tea

Now my fortunes are a-changing
I've won the lottery
And Nigel Butterworth's discovered
That he's in love with me

But you're too late Mr. Butterworth
You can beg a thousand pardons
I've made my bed of roses now
With Pete from Parks and Gardens

TRICK OR THREAT

I hate these Trick or Treaters
Who call round this time of year
Local yobs in hoodies
Who intimidate with fear

Last year when they knocked the door
I thought that I would mention
I can't afford to treat them
I just live on my pension

One wedged his foot inside my door
While the other little tyke
Broke into the shed and let
The tyres down on my bike

So this year I'll treat with chocolate
They won't believe their eyes
I've scooped out the middle layer
And substituted a surprize

They'll bite into the Mars bar
And when they start to chew
They'll find their nasty little gobs
Stuck up with super-glue

TWELVE GIFTS OF CHRISTMAS

Thank-you for the partridge
And the egg that it's just laid
And thank-you for the pear-tree
And the fancy gift-wrapped spade
I've only got a council flat
But I'll put it in a pot
It simply is delightful
And I like it – quite a lot

How kind and generous you are
Two turtle-doves arrived
They had a bust-up with the partridge
But, thankfully, it survived
They've settled down quite nicely
In the branches of the tree
How very thoughtful of you
To send such gifts to me

I can't believe it – three French-hens
My flat is full of birds
And I don't want to sound ungrateful
Or hurt your feelings with my words
But the pear-tree's buckling under
And I'm feeling quite unwell
I'm knee deep in bird droppings
And there's a really awful smell

Oh No, please not four calling-birds
I don't know what to do
The vet's condemned my council flat
And I've got avian 'flu
There're vicious little blighters
One gave me a nasty peck
And if I weren't humanitarian
I'd have wrung its scrawny neck

Now I want to end this friendship
I don't think that we're matched
Because as I write this letter
The blooming partridge egg has hatched
I've had a letter from the council
And the neighbour's in a rage
Why couldn't you just send me
A canary in a cage

I think I've been too hasty
Five gold rings – all eighteen carat
And I had an awful feeling
In the box there lurked a parrot
This gift's more to my liking
The inset diamonds played a part
To return you to my favour
And pave a pathway to my heart

I don't believe this morning's gift
I'm retracting what I said
I've six honking geese a-laying
On the duvet on my bed
Now the council's here to fumigate
There's been a signed petition
And a local deputation
Headed by a politician

You prat, you loon, you imbecile
What do you think you're doing
Seven swans a-swimming
Boy, have you got trouble brewing
They're paddling in the bathtub
And one's nesting in the sink
I've swallowed lots of tablets
But it's driving me to drink

The partridge hates the turtle doves
And in a beak and feather brawl
The French hens met their Waterloo
In the carnage up the hall
The calling birds stopped calling
And the geese no longer lay
I've drowned the swans a-swimming
I'll make sure you rue this day

Eight maids arrived a-milking
Jersey cows – a dairy herd
I've had to hire Clapham Common
Have you not heard a word
I've developed brucellosis
Drinking milk unpasteurised
And the sanitary inspector's
Been called round to sanitize

My nerves are all in tatters
Nine ladies dancing round a pole
My flat's reverberating
To the sound of rock and roll
The milk-maids hate the ladies
They're shocked and scandalized
I've had to call the doctor in
To have them tranquilized

Bad enough this manic dancing
Ten lords a-leaping in the throng
It's like a knocking-shop in Soho
With their wicked goings on
I've had the vice squad round here
My home's a flat of ill repute
You'll be hearing from my lawyer
As I intend to prosecute

Eleven pipers piping
With tartan kilts and swords
Have ravished all the ladies
And the flaming leaping lords
The council's called the social
The situation is absurd
They say they're going to put me
In a home for the disturbed

And now twelve drummers drumming
Can be heard from Bethnal Green
And they've brought along a plonker
Banging on a tambourine
But I'll get you, you rat-face
Somehow I'll make you pay
The ambulance has just arrived
And taken me away

TWELVE GIFTS RECYCLED

Waste not – want not is a motto
And now I am in the throes
Of recycling all the twelve gifts
That last year for me you chose

The partridge and its cheeper chick
In green fields released to fly
And the pear-tree bears its luscious fruit
Each Anno Domini

Two turtle doves I sent to Noah
And from the safety of his ark
They search for olive branches
To bring light where there is dark

Three French hens sent back to France
Though sad to see their exit
Can explain to European friends
Just why we voted Brexit

Four calling-birds with blackened wing
To grant freedom was a must
The Tudors liked their colly-birds
Baked crisply in a crust

I sold the five gold rings you sent
And the money I acquired
Will sit nicely in my bank account
Until the time that I'm retired

Six geese a-laying fed the hungry
But one laid an egg of gold
I'm hanging on to that old goose
The other five I sold

Seven swans a-swimming
On the Thames they can be seen
All ringed in the swan-upping
And belonging to the Queen

The maids a-milking Jersey cows
Each one of them – all eight
Applied for redeployment
And now work for Unigate

Nine naughty ladies dancing
In lace and sequinned gown
Are pirouetting round the night-clubs
With the low-life of the town

Ten lords a-leaping joined them
And to manic music sway
And the one without a partner
Swings the other way

I gave the piping pipers
To Her Majesty, the Queen,
And they took along the silly sod
Who banged the tambourine

Twelve drummers drumming madly
Enthusiastic but no skill
Went off to join the carnival
And disappeared in Notting Hill

So now my life is tranquil
And all is hunky-dory
I'm planning gifts to send to you
But that's another story

Watch this space

Yes – a baby partridge really is called a 'cheeper'

TWELVE GIFTS REVENGE

One year – twelve months – I've languished
But finally I have heard
That my release is imminent
From the home for the disturbed

My psychiatrist and therapist
Are quite prepared to vouch
That my mental state is balanced
And I'm wearing out their couch

I'm planning your comeuppance
And for you it's pay-back time
I'm turning your life up-side-down
Just like you did to mine

The first gift that I'll send you
Enough to turn you pale
One annual season ticket
For a train on Southern Rail

I've had a year to ponder
To take revenge, you loony lump
A treat that I've selected is
Two days with Donald Trump

I'm sending you **three** vultures
And a moulting golden eagle
I've called up bird protection
'Cos to keep them is illegal

The fourth gift that I've chosen
For you, you gormless chump
Four lengths of loose elastic
And a one-way bungee jump

I've got wives from dodgy web-sites
I'm now on the attack
Expect **five** from Mongolia
And each one brings a yak

Now I feel we're getting even
I'm settling the score
Along with five wives and their yaks
You'll get **six** Mothers-in-Law

I'll send **seven** Sergeant-Majors
That's enough to cause you trouble
For manoeuvers and square-bashing
And marching at the double

I've booked for you a holiday
Look forward to some fights
In Benidorm with lager louts
All **eight** on their stag nights

Nine nasty debt-collectors wait
With bailiffs at your door
You've fiddled all your Income Tax
And that's against the law

So expect **ten** Tax Inspectors
To go through your accounts
Said you've stashed your cash away
Off-shore – in huge amounts

I'm sending Traffic Wardens
Now how's this for a lark?
There's **eleven** waiting for you
Each time you try to park

And this my final gift to you
Now firmly we're estranged
Twelve months incarceration
In a home for the deranged

TWENTY-SIXTY-FOUR

The year two thousand and sixty-four
Saw great change in English Law
The making of men and women all equal
This was a popular law with the people
And lo and behold to women's delight
To give birth to babies became a man's right
Women were jubilant with this legislation
Let men enjoy the nine months gestation

So Freda married the man of her choice
The whole congregation was there to rejoice
Gave birth to the first child the following year
Without any fuss and barely a tear
But Freda was knowing and Freda was wise
And speaking to hubby with innocent eyes
Said "With the new law now I have reckoned
It must be your turn to give birth to the second"

So Norman, the name of the sweetheart she'd wed
With morning sickness soon took to his bed
His ankles were swelling, his man-boobs all sore
And nothing still fitted, whatever he wore
Freda called Norman her blossoming star
And went out and bought a maternity bra
Then on the internet, tapping the screen
Bought Mothercare vouchers and Boots Nipple Cream

"I'll not do it again, my decision is final
I spend most of the time in the flaming urinal
I've bloating and sweating and sex isn't an option
I'm beginning to wish we'd gone in for adoption"
And so Noman wished he'd not become equal
And campaigned to change the vote of the people
If Freda wants a third child then she can
But there won't be a fourth – not by me – I'm a man!

TWO-UP – TWO-DOWN

In a sad and dingy back-street
On the outskirts of the town
We came upon the old house
Two-up and just two-down

Looking for our first home
Somewhere quiet and residential
The Estate Agent described it as
'A dwelling with potential'

To renovate this hovel
We thought we'd have a bash
To make a home together
So we borrowed lots of cash

We got a cut-price ladder
Then bought ourselves some tools
Because the roof was leaking
And water running down in pools

We spent our days in B & Q
Searching up and down the aisles
Sorting out the bits and pieces
To fix leaky roofing tiles

The skirting boards were rotten
And the walls grew lots of mould
We hadn't any heating
So it was always freezing cold

We pulled up all the floorboards
And a million woodworm died
But the little mouse who lived there
We re-homed and he survived

Then we called the plumber
We had no plumbing skill
We lived on bread and water
To pay his blooming bill

Next came the electrician
To sort wire all bare and frayed
He ripped out our new skirting
And the floorboards we'd just laid

We hacked lime-scale off the toilet
And replaced the cistern chain
And painted with enamel
The bathtub's rusty stain

We white-washed all the ceilings
And polished up the floors
And in a cheerful yellow colour
We painted all the doors

We slashed away at nettles
And although the work was hard
We planted roses up a trellis
To adorn the old back-yard

So thanks to our endeavours
Our home is trendy – quite bijou
And with the price of houses
It's now worth a bob or two

So thank-you Estate Agent
We don't think of you with malice
Our two-up – two-down old house
Is now our little palace

UNWISE MOVE

Since the early sixties
From the day that we were wed
We saved up for a family home
Three reception and four bed

We've added an extension
And another bathroom too
Downstairs there's the kitchen
And we've got an extra loo

Now the Government's suggested
That OAP's should all down-size
To assist the housing market
But we've deemed that unwise

We could sell for something smaller
Put the surplus in the bank
But checking on the interest rate
We found it simply stank

Valuing our bricks and mortar
Increasing eight percent each year
It's a pretty sound investment
Will we sell it? – No darn fear

Does the Minister of Housing
While talking through his hat
Have a comfy home in London
Or a poky two-room flat

Will we decide to down-size?
I couldn't make it plainer
Trade eight for only one percent
Is a definite no-brainer

And while we're on the subject
I know this may sound mean
Will they be making this suggestion
To Her Majesty, the Queen?

WINDOWS OF THE NIGHT

From Amsterdam to Soho
In cities – Paris, New York, Rome
All have a red-light district
Which working girls call home

A girl of seventeen, no more
With painted face and coloured hair
Smiles her trade-seductive smile
But her eyes hold vacant stare

This girl who once had hopes and dreams
Which 'grooming' turned to dust
Now a price-list burned into her brain
For each perverted lust

From a sad and lonely childhood
Spent in a children's home
The 'groomers' on the internet
Chose her on which to hone

With drugs and drink and pretty things
The flash of city light
This evil gang of low-life
Lured to the darkness of the night

Subdued by fear and dominance
No chance of restitution
Broken by immoral men
To a path of prostitution

Shipped on out to Amsterdam
A commodity to trade
A child deprived by vice and greed
To feather nests of the depraved

And so she stands with hollow cheeks
To gaze with listless eyes
As the red light casts its ruby hue
On the punters she'll despise

Men will stop and stand and leer
Not see the tear upon her lashes
Just a body in the window
Bathed in the red-light flashes

Tutored well – this teenage siren
Forced by violence and fright
She strikes a pose and pops a pill
To face the windows of the night

WINTER SUNSHINE

I look out of the window
On dull cold winter days
I miss blue skies of summer
And the sunlight's golden rays

But the sun is always shining
And although the sky is grey
Look beyond the raindrops
And clouds there in the way

While we live our time together
'Til the sad day we must part
Let joy and love surround you
Keep the sunshine in your heart